Israel

The state of Israel is still in its infancy. Drawing upon the experience and expertise of established nations and, no less, upon its own spirit, it is building itself into a homeland for the Jewish people. At the same time, it cannot ignore those who are, or have become, Israeli not by choice, but through the circumstances of politics. In *We Live in Israel*, a cross-section of the Israeli people, whose families have uprooted themselves from homes throughout the world, tell you what their life is like – life on a kibbutz, life in the city, life in the desert.

Gemma Levine was born and educated in London and has homes in both London and Jerusalem, where she is a frequent visitor. This is her fourth book about Israel.

A BOOK IS A FRIEND

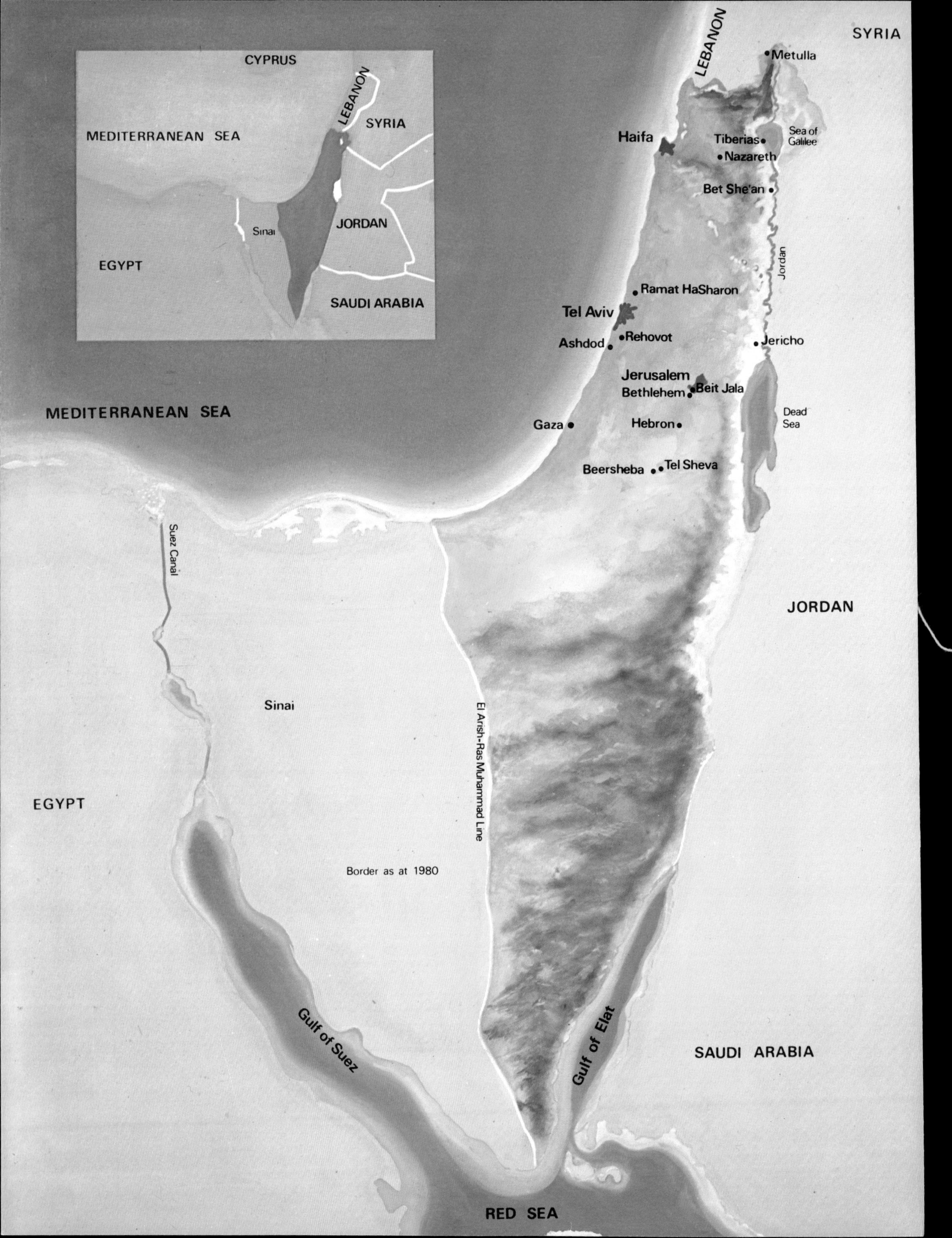

CYPRUS
LEBANON
SYRIA
MEDITERRANEAN SEA
Sinai
JORDAN
EGYPT
SAUDI ARABIA
LEBANON
SYRIA
Metulla
Haifa
Tiberias
Sea of Galilee
Nazareth
Bet She'an
Jordan
Ramat HaSharon
Tel Aviv
Rehovot
Ashdod
Jericho
Jerusalem
Beit Jala
Bethlehem
MEDITERRANEAN SEA
Gaza
Hebron
Dead Sea
Beersheba
Tel Sheva
Suez Canal
JORDAN
Sinai
El Arish-Ras Muhammad Line
EGYPT
Border as at 1980
Gulf of Suez
Gulf of Elat
SAUDI ARABIA
RED SEA

we live in
ISRAEL

Gemma Levine

Living Here

We live in Argentina
We live in Australia
We live in Brazil
We live in Britain
We live in Canada
We live in the Caribbean
We live in Chile
We live in China
We live in Denmark
We live in France
We live in Greece
We live in India
We live in Israel
We live in Italy

We live in Japan
We live in Kenya
We live in Malaysia and Singapore
We live in Mexico
We live in New Zealand
We live in Pakistan
We live in Poland
We live in South Africa
We live in Spain
We live in Sweden
We live in the U.S.A.
We live in the Asian U.S.S.R.
We live in the European U.S.S.R.
We live in West Germany

Further titles are in preparation

First published in 1981 by
Wayland (Publishers) Ltd
49 Lansdowne Place, Hove
East Sussex BN3 1HF, England

© Copyright 1981 Wayland (Publishers) Ltd

Second impression 1984

ISBN 0 85340 865 3

Phototypeset by Trident Graphics Ltd
Reigate, Surrey
Bound in the UK by The Pitman Press, Bath
Printed in Italy by G. Canale & C.S.p.A., Turin

Contents

Itzik Inbar, *kibbutznik*   6

Miri Alush, *university student*   8

Archimandrite Anthony Grabbe, *Dean of the Russian Orthodox Church*   10

Yael Avner, *voluntary worker*   12

D'wihi, *bedouin shaykh*   14

Mashtodz Parilouysian, *priest of the Armenian Church*   16

Achmad Abdaldia, *school messenger*   18

Gali Sabar, *soldier*   20

David Eylath, *executive*   22

Itzhak Nevet, *kibbutznik*   24

Muneir Baraket, *market shopkeeper*   26

Menashe Kadishman, *artist*   28

Lt.-Col. Touvia Navoth, *military commander*   30

Ettie Ben-Yaacov, *nurse*   32

Shabti Hermon, *rabbi*   34

Daniel Hendrickson, *recent immigrant*   36

Samuel Toledano, *politician*   38

Professor Daniel Cohen, *veterinary surgeon*   40

Michael Elkins, *BBC correspondent*   42

Yvonne Mattar, *headmistress*   44

Sadia Nahhas, *TV announcer/pharmacist*   46

Yehuda Lapidot, *university professor*   48

Benjamin Armon, *civil servant*   50

Miriam Bahar, *Youth Corps member*   52

Avram Hissan, *shop and factory owner*   54

Avraham Yoffee, *nature preservationist*   56

Eli Shalgi, *taxi driver*   58

Meir Ben-Dor, *archaeologist*   60

Israel fact sheet   62

Index   63

Glossary   64

'Jewish families have always stuck together'

Itzik Inbar, 35, was born in Haifa of parents who came to Israel from Poland. He became a kibbutznik at the age of 20. His wife Irit works in the kibbutz youth village 40 kilometres away.

As a youth, I was a member of a scout movement which directs its members towards kibbutz life. It was a natural continuation of the way I was brought up. By joining a kibbutz, I was able to fulfil the goals and principles of the scout movement in Israel, which are quite different from those of the scouts anywhere else in the world. It's a natural progression to go on to a kibbutz associated with your scout movement.

We work at least ten hours a day here, very often more. We have a very strong family life. Our afternoons are always spent with our children – this is a must for us. We begin work early in the morning just as the sun rises, and, because of the desert heat, we finish manual work at lunch-time. We have a small three-

Itzik and his family live in a typical kibbutz house, with three rooms.

roomed house and our children sleep with us; in some kibbutzim the children sleep together. In the evenings we usually have quite an active programme. Basically, we're a group of people with our own culture. There's a committee which organizes lectures, sports, arts and crafts.

Some 550 people live here, of whom 220 are 'members'. The children are not members. You have to choose to become a member. The fact that you are born here is no obligation – you're very welcome to become a member, but it isn't compulsory. Children usually become members when they reach eighteen or after they've completed their service in the army.

Youngsters usually return here to the kibbutz after their three-year army service. We believe very strongly that we must give to society. We believe our values and principles are higher than those in other societies, so our children stay away from the kibbutz an extra year after the army to involve themselves in general community service – some kind of social work. We don't want to separate ourselves from society.

Our children have been brought up in excellent conditions – the best education, stable economic conditions, but most important of all, they have a strong family life. We feel we can ask the young to do something for others. We think this is why our commune succeeds while others fail: we owe a duty towards the society outside. The work the young people do may be in a development town. It may be in a young kibbutz that needs help. On the other hand, some of the children use their free year to travel a little. If they need money for this, they work for six months to pay their way.

Schooling – in or out of the classroom – is an important aspect of kibbutz life.

Our kibbutz was established in 1965. We have a factory where we produce and sell drip irrigation systems. We call it the 'green revolution'; it has developed in the last ten years. In our system, irrigation is achieved with drippers and not sprinklers. We bring the water to the plant. There's no waste, no evaporation and just enough water is supplied to the plant.

We were the first to bring drip irrigation to Israel and were among the first production units in the world to convert what has been pure laboratory research into agricultural practice.

But the most meaningful part of kibbutz life is the importance of the family. Jewish families since way back have always stuck together. When the Holocaust came, it devastated families. I see today on the kibbutz lost tribes again being built up.

'This dream came true — it's miraculous'

Miri Alush is a 24-year-old university student born in Beersheba. She lives with her Tunisian-born parents, her nine brothers and six sisters. When she is not studying, she works in the Department of Social Workers attached to Ben Gurion University.

It was very difficult for my parents to raise and educate fifteen children. However, with the help of God they are managing. I went to school for eleven years, then joined the army for two years and now I'm a student of the Ben Gurion University here in Beersheba. At present I'm doing my pre-academic course to prepare for examinations. This university is unique in Israel: it accepts high-school students who have not completed their final studies. They prepare for their

The campus of Ben Gurion University: a dream come true.

The home of a large family is never empty, even when half the family is missing.

examinations here, so that a year later they can enter as first-year university students. I'm studying history and political science. I'm very interested in politics, and it's a happy coincidence that my father, who is in his late 50s, is also at this university studying the same subjects as I am.

Ben Gurion University was built about ten years ago. Before that, this area was just desert. It was Ben Gurion's dream to build a university and a cultural centre here in the middle of the desert – all Israel would be able to come and learn here. This dream came true. I think it's miraculous.

I study here three or four times a week, afternoons only. In the morning I work for the Department of Social Workers attached to the University. We call it 'open-apartments'. There are many problems. I'm given accommodation, a room, in return for working every morning with families. I look after their children; help them with their language problems and school work; and take them out of

their homes so that they can relax. The reason for this is that we have problems with the parents. They arrive as immigrants (from Morocco, for example) and they can't allow their children to be free. This causes many problems in the home, so my job is to help both parents and children to lead a more free and normal life.

I usually live at home with my family. As we're such a large family, the three eldest of us dress and feed the younger ones. I also help them with their homework. I'm not allowed to help my mother with the cooking. None of us really does housekeeping. She takes a great pride in her cooking – the family's favourite dish is couscous. But from time to time, when I get a little money, I buy clothes for the young ones or something new for the house. We all do our best and we're very happy.

'Being here enriches the spirit'

Archimandrite Anthony Grabbe is Dean of the Russian Orthodox Churches in the Middle and Near East. He was born in Yugoslavia of Russian parents.

My duties in the Holy Land are to take care of our schools, monasteries, convents and holy places; to co-operate with other Christian churches; and to attract more pilgrims to the Holy Land. It is also my job to extend the jurisdiction of our mission here in Israel.

My day is very busy: I'm here from early morning until late at night. I'm in charge of educational work in the United

The Russian Convent of St. Mary Magdalene in the Garden of Gethsemane.

States, and as there is seven hours time difference, I need to be here to receive telexes and give orders and advice – this goes on until eleven at night.

The Russian Convent of Ascension at the summit of the Mount of Olives houses 300 people – nuns, students, priests and teachers. We also have the Russian convent church of St. Mary Magdalene in the Garden of Gethsemane. There's another Russian convent in the hills of Ein Karem – among the orange groves and orchards in Jaffa; a chapel and hermitage in Wadi Faran by the Dead Sea; orchards near Jericho; the monastery and church near Hebron with the oak of Abraham; and the threshold stone of the Judgement Gate in Jerusalem, through which Jesus was led to Golgotha: all these are ours.

The threshold stone, which was bought by Archimandrite Antonin, is known as 'Russian Excavations'. While they were digging to lay foundations, the workers came upon remnants of the old market, a part of the city wall and the Judgement Gate. That part of the city wall still shows clear signs of the fire which brought down the Gate during the siege of Jerusalem by the ninth Roman Legion of the Emperor Titus in A.D. 70.

The ultimate pilgrimage, the life-long aspiration of many pious Christians has always been the long and hazardous voyage to the Holy Land. Slav people began their pilgrimages as early as the sixth and seventh centuries. The earliest written record of a pilgrimage to Jerusalem is that of a monk by the name of Vartaam, in the year 1062. In the following century a certain Russian, Abbot Daniel, left a detailed description of his journey to Palestine and of the holy

The building of the Russian Ecclesiastical Mission in Jerusalem. The Herodian pavement is in the foreground.

shrines he visited. He placed a vigil light at the Holy Sepulchre and lit it in the name of all Russia.

I believe that being here in the Holy Land enriches the spirit of both the young and the old. In my position here, I'm fully aware of the great challenge. I'm engaged in extensive programmes both in the United States and here in Israel. Most of my energies are involved in the restoration of the mission's and Society's legal rights; and in the preservation of religious shrines, historical landmarks and the precious cultural heritage of the civilized world.

'Women in uniform? Most unfeminine'

Yael Avner is 18 years old and lives with her English-born parents, Mimi and Gubby Avner, in an apartment in Jerusalem. She recently left school and is now working, awaiting her call-up into the army.

I went to school for twelve years, partly in America and partly in Israel. I was seventeen and a half when I left school after taking my matriculation exams. I took a short holiday and now I have eight months before I join the army. My first job was in a library. I worked in the acquisition department, where all the books are bought and then sorted for the university library. All I had to do was file and stack books. I was paid L.70 (£0.50) an hour.

As I was bored and the pay was bad, I left and took a job as a dental reception-ist, where I am now. I have to start work

. .

The calm blue waters of the Gulf of Elat are ideal for snorkelling.

Treasures of a natural kind, like these corals, await those who search the depths of the Red Sea.

at 8.30 a.m. and leave at 1.00 p.m. I make appointments, and have to smile at everyone. For this I get twice my old pay. My afternoons are spent with two new immigrant children, helping them with their homework and explaining a little of how the country is run. I earn a little from this too, so I can save what I earn from my morning job.

As I only work with the immigrants four afternoons a week, I have one free afternoon for voluntary work. I love babies, so I decided to work in the maternity section of a large hospital. I really enjoy the work. I wear a large white gown, and stand behind a window holding up new-born babies for families and visitors to admire. I work there for five hours.

The thought of going into the army worries me a little, but I'm looking forward to meeting new people, and to the adventure. It's only a two-year service for girls (three years for boys); it's compulsory, so I suppose we're resigned to it. The first three weeks will be the most difficult: there's an intensive course of physical training.

I hope to be a social worker in the army, trying to help soldiers with their problems. I'm not looking forward to wearing a uniform. It's awful for a girl. We have to wear large khaki shirts and very baggy trousers: most unfeminine. Our hair has to be up: no make-up at all; and huge, heavy boots. The worst part is getting up at four in the morning.

For relaxation, I adore Israeli folk dancing. I try to go every night of the week. I also love to read good classics. I make lists of books, but it isn't easy to find English translations of them all. Libraries are the best place to find them. Anyway, it's too expensive to buy new books. Television is not good here in Israel, so I don't watch too much. Luckily, I have other interests. I love camping holidays, going down into the Sinai desert with friends. Sometimes I go with my father. My mother hates going. We have great fun. Our days are spent snorkelling and the nights just watching the stars. I've become a keen astronomer. This is my Heaven.

13

'Our life is with the sheep and goats'

D'wihi is a Bedouin Shaykh. He was born in a tent in Abo Regaihik, a village near Tel-Sheva. He has two wives — he is looking for a third — and thirteen children.

My tribe is called Abuiack. The desert is divided up into tribal areas. In each area we have a limited water supply; the pasture and the right to cultivate the land belong exclusively to the tribe controlling that area. A bedouin tribe is a group claiming common possession over a certain territory. Each tribe knows the boundary of its land. I'm the head of my tribe; I was elected by the adult males to oversee their tribal interests.

My women make my tent from goat's hairs, woven together. These hairs expand when they're wet, making a watertight roof. In the summer they afford protection from the hot sun and desert sand-storms. The tent is divided by a woven curtain: one half is for the men and one half for the women. It's the natural home of the nomad. A tent is light; we can fold it up and put it on the back of a camel and move on.

Some bedouins have changed from the nomadic life to a settled life, and they prefer to live in buildings. Our life is

Hospitality is part of the desert culture. Passers-by are always offered refreshment.

The bedouin's life is still with the sheep and goats, wandering in search of new pastures.

with the sheep and goats, cultivating the earth: their life is now turning towards industry.

We send our children to school every day to learn. Some of our children will go on to university and will give up our traditional way of life. Camels used to be our only means of transport, but with the advent of trains and cars the camel has become less useful.

When we entertain, we cook a whole goat or a whole sheep. We make a fire and cook the animal in front of the guests. We, the men, eat the meat and we give the eyes and the brains to the women. We're always making strong black coffee or sweet tea to offer any passer-by at whatever time of day or night.

Our tent is our shelter. In Biblical times, Abraham received his guests in his tent. To this day, we have no greater pleasure than offering hospitality. It's part of our desert culture, even if it means sharing our last piece of bread.

My wife must be a Moslem bedouin. My mother will see her first and report back to me – whether she is good-looking; whether the economic situation of her family is good; whether she has gold – and then I decide if I want to marry her. I see her for the first time on our wedding day. In my position I can't have a cheap woman. (Women from the Gaza Strip are cheap.) Some bedouins still buy their brides for camels. Seven is considered a fair price. I like to marry someone from my family, as it strengthens the family unit. If I'm displeased with my wife, I can send her back to her family, but I have to pay for the upkeep of the children.

I am quite happy with two wives; I would like three, but four would be too expensive.

'Man must live by the word of God'

Mashtodz Parilouysian is a priest of the Armenian Church. Now aged 87, he was born in Musa Dagh, an Armenian mountain village. He came to Jerusalem as a refugee from Turkey, in 1933.

I came to the Holy Land on a pilgrimage. It was Easter when I came. I came on the day of the 'Holy Fire', Easter Saturday, the Holy Week. I stayed awake the whole night of the Fire. It was impossible to sleep that night because everyone around me was praying. It was always my dream to come to the Holy Land on that day.

Christ said you must make the choice

Choirboys of the Armenian Church bring further splendour to a solemn religious service.

Ceremonies in the Armenian Church provide a feast for the eye as well as the soul.

of me or the family. So I left my family and went to fulfil my dreams. When I was seventeen and at school, I read that, if you marry, you either have the choice of God or a wife. So to please God, I was to serve him, and run from the other way of life. Everyone is endowed with the grace of God. I don't have the pride of being educated, but I am pious, and happy with being pious.

From an early age I used to read the Bible – the Prophets. The Prophets slept and prayed for the whole world, so every day I do this.

Before becoming a priest, I served in the Holy Sepulchre as a sacristan and night deacon. I woke up 365 nights of every year for ten years to say mass on 'The Tomb of the Lord' (Jesus).

Why did I choose this uncomfortable way of life at that time? It was my love for the Lord. In 1946 I was ordained a priest. Then I became the Superior of The Holy Sepulchre for nine years. From

that period until now I have been Father Confessor of the community.

My mother gave me this advice: if you live a spiritual life, you stay healthy. I keep reading the history of the hermits, especially Daniel, who used to fast; eating and drinking is for a worldly life. Eating should be honest, only to keep the body alive. I awake at 4.00 a.m. At 11 o'clock I begin to pray for the world, every day. Then I sleep afterwards, and wake at four and go to church, even if I'm sick. I feel I am not worthy of eating my daily bread if I don't go to church every day.

Man does not live by bread but by the word of God. There is worldly wisdom and there is heavenly wisdom. People go by the worldly wisdom. The fact that there are problems is because people do not go by heavenly wisdom.

'We are known for our beautiful flowers'

Achmad Abdaldia is a 50-year-old refugee who lives in Jericho. He was born in Selamie Village in Palestine and came to Jericho in 1948, after the War. He now works as a school messenger, and is married with ten children.

I am now living here in Jericho in a refugee camp which houses 3,000 people. Most of the other people left for Jordan after the War when the Israelis came here to Jericho in 1967. The United Nations Relief and Works Agency (U.N.R.W.A.) built a school here in the camp and they are providing me with my job, my clothes and my food. Everything. They look after me and my family, and they give me a small salary for my work at the school. I start my work here at 5.00 a.m. and work until 4.00 p.m.

The Monastery of St. George nestles amongst the rocks in Wadi Kelt, above Jericho.

The comforts of an Arab refugee camp are few. Home is four walls and a roof.

I have three rooms in my house. The ten children sleep in two rooms. They are very happy. All the children go to school. There are three schools in the camp and U.N.R.W.A. provides us with clothing and food for the children. Not all the families live as we do. Many of the people from the camp work in the factories in Israel. Their salaries are brought out from Israel.

I grow vegetables for the family to eat – onions and potatoes. We get our water from a large communal pool. We collect it ourselves in buckets. There's a monastery nearby, in Wadi Kelt up in the Judean Desert above Jericho, called The Monastery of St. George. There's a stream there that runs down the mountains and collects into a pool near our house. The donkeys drink from the pool; the women wash their clothes there; and we take all our drinking water from the pool. Chemicals are added to the water to make it pure. We have enough water throughout the year, even though it's always very hot and humid here. We are 250 m (820 ft) below sea-level.

Flowers grow very readily here. We are known for our beautiful and richly-coloured poincianas, which line our streets. We also grow bananas, mangoes, pomelos (grapefruit), date palms and other tropical fruits. It must have been paradise when Herod reigned and Cleopatra's balsam gardens were in full bloom.

19

'I feel ready to shoulder responsibilities'

Gali Sabar is 19 and lives in Tel Aviv. Her parents are Israeli. Gali is completing her two years' service in the army and is based in the Negev, south of Beersheba.

As it's Friday afternoon, I shall go home to my family. We live in an apartment in Tel Aviv. I usually go home for Sabbath and rest for the day; on Sunday I have to return to my army base in the Negev. Sometimes my duties prevent me from getting home.

I don't mind my studies being interrupted by compulsory army service. I love the army. We meet people from all

A view of Haifa. Gali is getting to know both the geography and the people of Israel through her army service.

walks of life – everyone is interesting. I find my work enjoyable and not too arduous. I've already been in the army a year. Girls do only two years' service, while boys serve for three years. I'm doing something special. On Friday we get our weekly programme. We guide soldiers around Israel to acquaint them with the country. We also have to show them special routes which they might need to use in the future.

We're already used to the feel of the army – boys and girls alike – from the scout movement and then the *Gadna*. We don't feel much tension.

The only time I carry a gun is when I visit the West Bank area of Gaza, or when I'm alone in Jerusalem. I'm afraid I can't tell you what sort of guns we carry. It doesn't bother me at all to carry one – I feel protected. Most of the time we don't need one.

Every three months we have five days off. But when we're in camp we usually get up at 6 o'clock. We have breakfast and then go to the office. We start our tour for the day and get back to camp in the evening. After dinner there are educational activities – lectures and so on. Often we have a camp fire; we really enjoy singing traditional Hebrew and army songs.

I'm a vegetarian, so the army diet is good for me. For breakfast we have eggs, bread, cheese, jam and some kind of vegetable. For lunch we're generally given meat (I have cheese and vegetables), potatoes, spaghetti, rice, fruit and drink. The evening meal consists of starchy food – often hot potatoes and a repeat of our breakfast menu.

I studied biology and mathematics at school. After my service in the army, I

The desert provides a dramatic backdrop to the gruelling army manoeuvres.

want to go to university and study medicine.

So far my training has taught me a great deal. I'm now getting to know the country like the back of my hand. I also get to know people better – people I wouldn't normally have the occasion to meet. I'm also far more aware of the problems of the country and have benefited from the strong army discipline. Now I feel ready to shoulder more responsibilities and set a personal example. I think far more independently than before and I have much more self-confidence.

'On the wings of the eagle'

David Eylath, 58, is Manager Community Relations and Deputy Secretary General of El Al Israel Airlines. He was born in Lwow, Poland, and moved with his parents to Israel in 1936.

El Al has six jumbos, two 737s, seven 707s and eight 747s – we could cope with a few more. Our planes are not manufactured in Israel, of course. They're built in Seattle, in the U.S.A. After the establishment of the State of Israel in 1948, the Government decided to create its own airline. But the purpose of the airline was different from other airlines. It was born through the need to bring home to Israel the Jews from Yemen and other Arab countries. A number of planes were bought, a company was formed, and a unique operation began which, as time went by, became known as 'The Magic Carpet', carrying thousands of Jews from remote places – some of whom had, until then, been living in caves.

A flight on El Al is often more of a social occasion than a mere journey.

At first we were worried about how these people would react to western civilization. We wondered whether they would even agree to board the planes. Wouldn't they be afraid? But we could not have been more wrong. Because the Jewish Yemenites were very religious, they had studied the Bible; they read and wrote Hebrew, the universal language of the Israelites. And in the Bible, in the Prophets, one can find many passages referring exactly to what was happening: 'Fear not, says the Lord, for I am with thee: I will bring thy seed from the east and gather thee from the west: keep not back. Bring thy sons from far and thy daughters from the ends of the earth. But they shall fly upon the shoulders of the Philistines towards the west: and I shall bring thee to the promised land on the wings of the eagle.'

These planes which came to fetch them, with a crew that spoke Hebrew – the language of the Bible – were the 'big eagles' mentioned by the Prophets. In flight a problem developed – a few of the passengers wanted to start a bonfire to make some coffee, just as they were used to doing in the desert.

As the airline of the people of Israel, we are promoting the Land of Israel. We welcome tourists to see the Land of the Ancient and the New: the biblical and historical sights; the *kibbutzim* and the *moshavim* (co-operative settlements); the industry; the beauty of the land – Jerusalem, Haifa, Tel Aviv; and (most of the time) the sunshine.

Then there are the four seas: the blue Mediterranean; and the Sea of Galilee – we call it *Kinneret*. It has the shape of a violin. At night, when the wind is blowing, you can hear violins playing. The Red Sea – it should have been the Sea of

One of El Al's fleet of twenty-three Boeings, all manufactured in Seattle, U.S.A.

Reeds (in Hebrew *Yam Soof*), but when the red mountains of Edom reflect in the sea, it really becomes red. The Dead Sea, which is no longer dead – it gives life to many people. We now extract phosphate, bromide, salts and other minerals from it, and thousands of tourists go there to take special sulphur mud baths at the natural springs. All this gives health and life.

But most of all if you are coming to Israel, meet its people, get to know them, learn about their striving for peace and friendship. And when you come, don't see Israel only with your eyes – see it with your heart.

When you see the faces of Jewish people at airports whenever an El Al plane lands, and you see their reaction to the Star of David on the blue and white Israeli flag, only then can you understand why El Al is different from other airlines.

'I speak to people through my flowers'

Itzhak Nevet, now 65, was born in Poland and settled in Palestine in 1934. He, his wife, their four children and their grandchildren all live on a kibbutz which specializes in the cultivation of orchids.

I left Poland in 1934. We left illegally for Palestine as there weren't enough certificates for the pioneers. We were caught, so we stayed at sea for six months. Eventually we escaped, went back to Poland and were later given papers to leave the country for Palestine. I came here at the age of eighteen.

My first wife was murdered by the Arabs. She left me one child, who is here at the kibbutz. My present wife had been widowed through an air crash; she has two daughters. Now we have a child of our own.

Before we came to this kibbutz, we lived in a temporary home (tents and barracks) in Rehovot. The first settlers came here in 1936. At that time I went to a kibbutz in the Jezreel valley to learn how to work in the fields and to see for myself how a kibbutz functions. It was in that year the Arabs began to riot. They wanted to stop us building, so they bombarded the roads.

Our initial work was to blast stones to

Itzhak cross-breeds plants to produce new varieties.

provide building materials, to dig foundations and to plant trees, which have
flourished into the pine forests which
you can now see. At night we defended
the place by force. That was the period
which we called the 'fence and tower'.
During the summer we bored holes ready
to plant. We waited for the rains and
then planted. Five people were doing the
work. One day they were ambushed by
the Arabs and killed. We continued our
work to establish this kibbutz in their
memory. In 1938 we began to live here.

I always worked with plants. It's not
only a profession, but a love. My orchids
are sent to Europe. They are exported
with agricultural products, flowers and
honey by a large company called
AGREXO. They have a centre in Germany
where they receive the orders. These are
not the only flowers that I experiment
with. There are also tulips. I had to discover what conditions I could work with.
For example, you can't grow corn, wheat
or other grain here, as the land is rocky.
So I had to decide on a more intensive
crop.

I cross-breed to change the nature of
plants, in the same way as you can cross
two different varieties to make a new
fruit or vegetable. Once I had gained
experience, cultivating orchids became
easier. Every man who is experienced in
a nursery has his favourite plants. We are
very famous for our orchids – some are
new varieties. There are only two or
three other orchid nurseries in this country.

There is an accepted international pro-
cedure for naming crossed flowers.
There are forms to fill out and so on: an
official process. I look after my orchids
almost twenty-four hours a day; even at
night I'm packing the orchids to send

*Itzhak's kibbutz is famous in Israel for the beau-
tiful orchids it produces.*

away, or checking the equipment.

Flowers are a medium through which I
can speak to the people. You came to see
the flowers before you came to see me.

'I have one prayer – for peace'

Muneir Baraket, 31, owns a shop in David Street, in the Arab Market. Like his parents, he was born in Jerusalem. He has bought a second home in Jericho, where the family spend their week-ends and holidays.

I live in the Moslem quarter in Jerusalem. Within the old city walls there are four quarters: the Moslem, Christian, Jewish and Armenian districts. Some 11,000 Christians, mostly Arabs, live in Jerusalem, and most of the sects have their headquarters in this area. It's quite a large area; we can walk for hours through the dark lanes and vaulted markets – an inheritance we have gained from

The Dome of the Rock, which no tourist to Jerusalem would fail to visit.

Crusader days.

All my free time is spent with my family. We've bought a second home in Jericho – a large house with three bedrooms, living room, bathroom, kitchen and a garden. We go there every weekend and for our holidays. It's very warm there in winter, while it's cold here. It's extraordinary; Jericho is only three-quarters of an hour away from Jerusalem and yet there is a total change of climate.

My wife loves to cook and we give a lot of parties. We like to cook a whole lamb and stuff it with rice; it's cooked in a large copper pot. We spend several hours over a meal with guests.

You can find many different types of wares in these markets: glass blown in Hebron; engraved metal plates; bowls; jugs from Iran and Arabia; ebony and mother-of-pearl boxes, and furniture from Damascus; woven rugs; and fine Persian carpets from Shiraz and Isfahan. I sell all these things in my shop. We also sell some very beautiful hand-embroidered dresses from the bedouins, who are always coming to sell us their wares. People can also buy their daily supplies here – groceries of all kinds: nuts, vegetables, fruit, *laben* (balls of hard white cheese in olive oil), sweet cakes with sesame seed. There's a meat market, a spice market, many clothes markets, and markets for sheepskins and basketry.

We sell mostly to tourists. We try to be very hospitable, and serve our customers with sweet tea with *nana* (mint) and sweet Turkish coffee. We even invite our customers to our own homes to meet the family. I speak English, Arabic, Hebrew and French. I learnt them all at school. Now, of course, I use them every day.

Our day is very long. We open the

A lady carries her purchases from the Arab market in a basket on her head.

shop at 8 a.m. and work through until six at night. We're Moslem, but we even work during Ramadan, except at prayer-time, which we observe five times a day. We can't eat during the day, but we have a feast at night. I pray near here at the silver-domed El-Aqsa Mosque. Nearby is the Dome of the Rock, where I also pray. It's so beautiful with its façade of gleaming gold and cut marble and brightly coloured glazed mosaics. A Moslem legend tells that an indentation in the rock surface marks Mohammed's footprint. Above it is a casket holding hairs from the prophet's beard; this is opened every year on the twenty-seventh day of the Feast of Ramadan.

I have only one prayer and that is for peace.

'From nature to art – art to nature'

Menashe Kadishman is a 49-year-old artist living in Tel Aviv. He studied art in Israel and at St. Martin's and the Slade School of Fine Art, London. He holds one-man exhibitions in Europe and the U.S.A.

As a child, I was asked to paint our young people's holiday buildings in wonderful, bright, cheerful colours; we called the buildings 'our nest'. Then I became interested in painting and began to study art in school, and also spent much of my time with some of our leading artists. I learnt so much from them, and that proved to be a very good grounding for me. But then my love of Israel took me into the country to see nature in the widest sense – shape, form, colour and so on.

Menashe stands amongst his painted sheep on the Tzora kibbutz.

As a young boy, I went to Negev, in the south, to the copper mines. It was full of stones, rocks, wonderful rich colours, huge shapes and landscapes. At the time I just couldn't work there: it was so overpowering. Only later when I came to London was I able to produce sculpture from memory.

Then, as now, I loved to wander as a shepherd through the hills and valleys of the Bible – the Jezreel valley, Mount Gilboa, Mount Carmel and the River Jordan. It's so rewarding to roam around and to recall from biblical times the founders of our nation, the patriarchs Abraham, Isaac and Jacob. They, too, wandered the length and breadth of the land with a staff in their hand, a knotted stick from the branch of an oak.

As I have an inborn love of nature and animals, I went to live on a kibbutz in that area. Walking through the hills day by day with the sheep, I grew to love the animals and have since become known for my drawings and paintings of sheep. At the Venice Biennale I even presented sheep from my kibbutz with their backs painted, applying my art to real nature.

I remember walking on those very hills where David cursed the mountains (Mount Gilboa) after Jonathan was killed because they weren't fertile and were arid. I felt, and feel, very much involved with the sentiments of the Bible and with my heritage. I felt the right thing, for me, was to work with the sheep, as I'd identified so strongly with them. I do believe that art doesn't have to be hung on walls; that's why I painted on the sheep as shepherds do. For example, when a sheep is pregnant, it's dabbed with blue; if it has an injection of a certain kind, it's dabbed with pink, and so on. It's not a gimmick: I believe nature

Amram's Pillars. Menashe found such dramatic landscapes overpowering.

and art can be merged together and be beautiful.

It began when we had an exhibition here, at the Israel Museum, *From Nature to Art and Art to Nature*. I also did a project on cut-out trees. Because of the climate, the trees in this country are so varied. My interest in trees started when I was a child. I was taught to plant trees – in those days forests were non-existent. Now our country, particularly in the north, is massed with trees and forests. Naturally, down in the desert trees are few and far between. There's the acacia tree, which shields both people and animals from the midday sun, and the tamarisk, which is one of the few trees that grows in extreme heat. As part of my work, I actually paint on the trees, as well as making sculpture cut-out trees that I place in the water so that the waves come through the holes. Again, nature to art – art to nature.

'Our worst enemy is a detonator'

Lieutenant Colonel Touvia Navoth is the military commander of the sub-district of the Jordan Valley under the military command of Judea and Samaria. He is 51 years old and has been stationed on the Allenby Bridge for six years.

The Allenby Bridge is one of two bridges which span the waters of the Jordan River. One and a quarter million people cross over these two bridges every year. This is called the 'open bridge' policy. It has been general practice since 1967 to allow commercial goods, mainly agricul- tural and building materials, to cross, as well as people from the West Bank. It's a little different for people going back the other way into Jordan. They are usually students studying in various Arab coun-

All vehicles that cross the Allenby Bridge must be thoroughly checked.

tries, diplomats and clergy. If you take into consideration that none of them is friendly to Israel, you will realize that one of our major jobs is security checking – almost 5,000 people daily on two bridges. In the summer months the temperature can be over 100 degrees Fahrenheit (38°C). We have to make body checks, and papers have to be checked to ensure that the person has been authorized to cross and that this is registered in his passport.

We must also check that any packages he might carry are clean. I mean clean: our worst enemy is a detonator measuring $1\frac{1}{2}$ cm × 4 mm ($\frac{1}{2}$ in by $\frac{1}{16}$ in). We also have to check luggage. We have tourists crossing from abroad and they too have to be checked, not because we think that an American might bring across explosive charges from Jordan. Someone in his hotel the previous night could have known he was going to cross into Israel the next morning. Something could easily have been planted in his luggage.

The bridges are open six days a week from 7 a.m. until dark. We work after the bridge is closed at night for three to four hours to check the last people that have crossed. Because we're in a border area, the terminal remains open. In spite of all the security checks we have to carry out, we do try to conserve the dignity of those we search. It's quite difficult to do this when you're asking them to undress down to their underwear. We have women checking women and babies, and men checking men.

People aren't allowed to import things that can't be checked thoroughly, so they know that any goods that can't be checked must either be destroyed or sent back unopened to Jordan.

Lt.-Col. Navoth has been stationed on the Allenby Bridge for the past six years.

'Not enough nurses, but we manage'

Ettie Ben-Yaacov is a 34-year-old nurse. She served in the army during the Six Day War and decided to specialize in army nursing. Now she is in charge of the emergency ward at Haddasa Hospital, Ein Karem.

I completed my training as a nurse at the Haddasa Nursing College here. Then I went into the army and served in the Six Day War. Because of the experience I gained, I decided that I would specialize in army nursing. After the war in 1968 I came straight to the hospital here and offered my services in the emergency ward. During the last war I was sent into the field to work with the army for six months.

Our day is very hectic. I begin at 7.30 in the morning and work until about 5 o'clock, depending on the number of emergencies we have to cope with. I'm on call most nights and sometimes I have to work through the night.

We have an agreement with the army to accept soldiers. We're the only hospital in this area of Jerusalem with such an arrangement. The soldiers are transported to us either by helicopter or by army ambulance, sometimes from very far away. We're on duty every day for head and chest surgery.

Every ward is equipped with modern

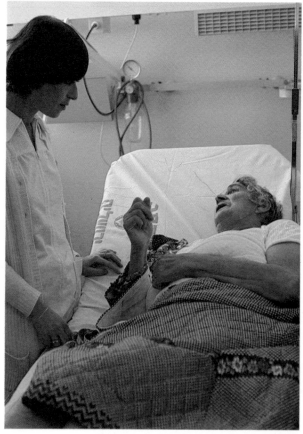

A nurse on an emergency ward must offer 'tender loving care' as well as her skills.

The beauty of Ein Karem can only speed the recovery of the post-operative patients.

facilities. Emergency doctors and specialists can be called from anywhere in the hospital at a moment's notice.

We don't have enough nurses, but somehow we manage – the patients don't know this. Sometimes families take their relatives upstairs to the X-ray room if they wish and if they know the way, but we don't allow them to take them into the operating theatre.

I love to listen to music and read, but after a day here I'm tired – I don't get home until 6 or 7 o'clock at night.

I've just received a 'phone call: a message came through from the American Embassy. They're sending a child by plane from Cairo; he was involved in a car accident. This is typical. We get many casualties from Jordan, from Cairo, from the United Nations very often.

We have about 700 beds here; it's not one of our larger hospitals. But we're lucky with our position here, right up in the hills of Ein Karem; it's one of the most beautiful sights in Israel. As soon as our patients have had their operations, once they look out over the hills, they can't help but be on the road to recovery. The hospital staff create a very good atmosphere and always seem cheerful. This makes working here not only rewarding, but also a pleasure. There's no other job for me.

'It's here that the Messiah will come'

Shabti Hermon is a 37-year-old Rabbi who works and lives at the Diaspora Yeshiva, an institute for religious instruction, on Mount Zion, Jerusalem. He was born in Cape Town, South Africa, but his family originally came from Lithuania.

I first came to Israel in 1961; my sympathies attracted me to the land of Israel. After I had been here some years, I began to develop an interest in religion and joined the Diaspora Yeshiva on Mount Zion in Jerusalem. I'm there now and have been for the past seven years.

The Diaspora Yeshiva is a unique institution. It was founded by a rabbi from New York in 1967. The Yeshiva

'The Messiah will come right over the Mount of Olives. The Mount of Olives will split open.'

Students of the Diaspora Yeshiva study the Gemara, the spoken laws of Judaism.

provides a framework for those with no religious background at all in their life to come and study the *Torah* and live according to the teachings of the *Torah*. The Yeshiva is conducted in the most orthodox of fashions. The standard of study is very high; we engage mainly in an in-depth study of *Gemara*, which is the spoken laws. This is the traditional Jewish form of study which goes back thousands of years. The Yeshiva is unique in that it enables a person with very little knowledge of our religion, if any, to develop himself and become a scholar. His development need have no limit. It's a great intellectual challenge. We don't treat him as a baby when he joins us, but already as an intelligent, advanced student.

We have accommodation here for twenty-two married couples, and another forty-five rooms for single, male students. Those we cannot accommodate live in the Jewish quarter a few minutes walk from here. We also have our women's division and dormitory in the Jewish quarter.

It's here on Mount Zion that the Messiah will come. We can see the Mount of Olives from here: the Messiah will come right over the Mount of Olives. The Mount of Olives will split open; there will be a flood in this valley which lies here at the foot of Mount Zion and the Messiah will enter through the Gate of Mercy, the Golden Gate, into the Temple.

The *Talmud* tells us that the Messiah would come if there were just ten Jews sitting together and devoutly studying the *Torah*. This is our role here at the Yeshiva, to develop wise students of the *Torah* – both through their learning and their way of life – to be like those ten people. Through their studies and their way of life, they will bring the Messiah and see the re-building of the third Temple in our days.

'A wonderful beginning to a new life'

Daniel Hendrickson, 41, has just arrived in Israel from the U.S.A. and lives in Mevaseret Zion, an absorption centre. He, his wife and his children have been provided with housing for the first few months.

The main reason for our coming to Israel is that we wanted the children to grow up not only knowing that they were Jewish, but also in a Jewish environment. We felt that just having a Jewish home in America was not enough. So we made a final break with the States in order to spend the rest of our lives here in Israel.

The absorption centre is owned by the Jewish Agency. Every family has their own two- or three-bedroomed house with their own kitchen, so we eat meals with our own family. We've had very full days during the short time we've been here at the centre. We begin our day at

Every family has its own house, so there is no interruption in the development of family relationships.

six, send the children off to school by seven, and by 8 o'clock we are in our Hebrew class, which lasts until 1.00 p.m. After that, we do our household duties – laundry, shopping etc. We have a laundry and supermarket here on the premises.

My wife and I have become very active in the singing and music world in Jerusalem, not far from here. We love opera, and take part in chorus rehearsals most evenings. I'm also a member of a choir and attend rehearsals for that too. So our evenings are fully occupied. For the children there are structured programmes in art, gymnastics and various other recreational activities. They also study music. Like ours, their day is very full.

In America I worked for the Federal Government in an agency that dealt with social problems. My first feelings were that I wanted to do the same type of work here, but now I'm pursuing some side lines in real estate and life insurance, plus my singing which I'm doing professionally. I'm finding that what were my side lines in the States might well become my main activity here. So I might not get back in to social work at all.

We have some savings, which makes life a lot easier for us than perhaps for some Russians who arrive with just their clothes on their backs. We have also had a little help from the Jewish Agency, which will probably cover our food bills. This will last for five or six months. After that, if I'm not working, I can claim employment compensation, which again is just enough for food. Unless you come here as a refugee, it's best to have a bit of capital behind you.

The purpose of the *Ulpan* is strictly to

The absorption centre gives immigrants the opportunity to learn the language and culture of their new country.

promote the study of the Hebrew language. But with the study of its language, you learn so much of the history and geography of the country. We're given trips and tours to all parts. Now we've been almost everywhere. This is part of the absorption process; when you've seen most of the country, it helps you to know where you would like to settle.

I don't think we have ever been as happy as we are here. We have a feeling of fulfilment. We meet people like us, coming to live here, from all over the world. It's a wonderful beginning to a new life.

'We're going through a difficult period'

Samuel Toledano is a 59-year-old member of the Knesset – Israel's parliament. His family originally came from Toledo in Spain, but he himself was born in Tiberias in Galilee.

From 1952 until 1966 I was in the *Mosad*, the Israeli C.I.A. They deal with three basic problem areas: intelligence gathering in Arab countries; tracking down wartime Nazis such as Eichman; and bringing Jews to Israel from countries it is difficult for them to leave.

In 1966 I was appointed as an advisor on Arab affairs and in that capacity I worked for different Prime Ministers,

Golda Meir, Rabin and Eshkol. I was elected to Parliament in 1977 and became the chairman of the State Control Committee.

Half a million Arabs fled from Palestine in the 1948 War of Independence. Some 155,000 remained in Israel and became Israeli Arabs holding Israeli

Samuel Toledano was born in Galilee. Lake Kinneret is one of the region's beauty spots.

passports and enjoying full Israeli citizenship. We have Arabs in Parliament. For the first time in the history of the Jewish nation we were a majority having to deal with an Arab minority. Unfortunately, though, Israel is fighting the Arab world. It's in a state of war with all the Arab countries other than Egypt. The deputy Arab Minister (Abdul Aziz Azoni) put it well: 'My country is fighting my people, the Arab people, and this is my tragedy.' I think the Arabs in Israel face a real dilemma, wanting to be good Israelis and yet good Arabs as well. It's practically a mission impossible. It is very difficult to be loyal to both sides while they're fighting each other.

The Jewish population, some three million Jews, are also facing their own dilemma. They have to integrate half a million Israeli Arabs within the State, economically, politically and socially. Again, it's not easy to fight some of the Arabs and integrate the others. But after thirty-two years of co-existence between the Jews and Arabs living here, I think that Israel is successful. Jews and Arabs live together in Haifa, Jaffa and Jerusalem. They have political problems and difficulties, but on the whole I think we have succeeded – at least, to this day.

The young Israeli Arab born in Israel has a new and special identity. He is very different from his brother on the West Bank – much more like a Jew of Tel Aviv. But on the other hand, he still feels himself part of the Arab nation. He wants a Palestinian State. The Arabs have a very high birth-rate. The problems they face today are mainly those of the intellectual Arabs; we call them the Arab sabras. We now have about 120,000 young Arab intellectuals going to schools and universities.

The seat of the Israeli parliament – the Knesset – in Jerusalem.

Those who were born in this country, who have never been under the British Mandate, try hard to adapt themselves to the new situation of living in a new state, finding jobs, including those in government offices. On the other hand, they must not betray their own people. They are exempted from military service and national service. Both the government and they themselves came to the conclusion that it was impossible to ask brothers to fight against each other. We're going through a difficult period. We hope that within a few years we'll be at peace with Arab countries and that we shall have Arabs as our Ambassadors abroad, Arabs in the Cabinet and Arabs sharing the leadership of this nation.

'Nobody was interested in the camel'

Professor Daniel Cohen was born in Brooklyn, New York, and is now 56 years old. A veterinary surgeon, he is the Israeli authority on the treatment of camels, and established a special camel clinic in 1978.

My main work here in this modern compound in the middle of the desert has been related to the interaction of human and animal diseases, and the contribution that veterinary medicine can make to human health and welfare. I also study population medicine, which is what epidemiology is all about: how groups of people adapt; how the environment influences them; and how this relates to human health.

This is a centre for comparative medicine – the study of those diseases in animals which reflect a similar human disease. There are some 320 animal diseases that are the mirror image of similar human conditions. It's possible to study these diseases and learn from them something about how human beings will react to similar conditions. So this hospital was established as part of a centre to study the occurrence of certain diseases in animals – cancer, liver, kidney or skin diseases. All these occur in animals and we are interested here to see whether diseases that occur in animals in the desert occur more or less frequently in the same animals in other environments. That is what we mean by comparative medicine.

In addition, there are some 200 diseases in animals which are naturally transmitted to man. Infectious diseases,

What better place for a camel clinic than the middle of the desert?

The beast of burden is afforded rest in the mid-day heat of the desert.

parasitic diseases, the sort of thing you can catch from your domestic pet or from wild animals. Here again, we are trying to discover which of these many diseases will prove to be a problem for us as we settle the deserts. Some of these diseases occur naturally in the desert. We only discover them when man comes to the region with his animals and comes into contact with insects or wildlife.

Other diseases are brought by humans to the desert – or by the animals which they bring with diseases that have never occurred here before.

We opened the first camel clinic in 1978. Because of our location, we were naturally in close contact with the bedouins. So we found that we were taking care of their goats and sheep. We discovered that while the government was interested in the goats and sheep because they provide food for humans, nobody was interested in the camel, because it is only a work animal for the bedouins.

Although many people in the Arab world have written about the camel, there has been no complete systematic study of the animal. Next year we're producing the first anatomical atlas of the camel. There are between fifteen to eighteen billion camels in the world. We are also engaged in the study of their diseases.

The camel is an animal which has not been utilized to the full. Not only does it give meat and milk, but it's also a beast of burden. But what is more important, it's an animal which is adapted to large areas of the earth where other animals can hardly survive. There's a growing interest in utilizing the camel as an animal that won't destroy the ecological system and yet can serve as an increasingly important source of meat and milk. The problems are essentially veterinary because the animal suffers from a number of genetic diseases. Until these are brought under control, the animal can't properly be developed and used for its meat and milk. We're trying to create the most modern clinic for camels and to make it an international centre for this important research.

41

'The gun, the bomb, the bullet'

Michael Elkins, 64 years old, is the BBC correspondent in Israel. Born in New York, he now lives in the heart of Jerusalem. His son, Johnathan, aged 25, is studying computer engineering at university.

I arrived in Israel with my wife in 1948. We came on a ship from New York with 1,400 immigrants. I was the security officer. After the 1948 war, we left to return to the U.S.A. but found life there was too pallid for us, so we came back to be in on the 'birth of Israel'.

The only way I could find to make a living was to start work in documentary films. I went to Yemen during 'Operation Magic Carpet' (bringing in the Yemeni Jews) and then worked on my first film, *Flight to Freedom*. Never before had I seen these tribes of Moroccans and Yemenites. I realized then that I had a bond with every Jew in the world.

I never meant to be a journalist. I

Sabra, the fruit of the cactus, is also the name for an Israeli-born Jew – prickly on the outside and soft within.

became a BBC correspondent quite by accident – purely as someone asked to fill a gap.

I decide late at night, or very early in the morning, to do a broadcast. I rise well before 6.00 a.m., skim through the newspapers, and listen to the Hebrew news broadcast. Then I decide what is the major story of the day and whether I have something to add, my thoughts or analysis. If I think I have an extra dimension to offer, then I gulp down some coffee to wake myself up, and settle down to write the piece, which I then read over the telephone. I'm always fully aware that I'm speaking and reaching out into millions of homes, so I'm very conscious of the importance of every word. I'm a deeply committed Jew and Zionist, but I must be totally fair: this haunts me all the time.

As the day begins, I talk with many people, from all walks of life, and learn what's going on and what the day's stories are. Unfortunately, my job is to report the gun, the bomb, the bullet – violence. We never do get to report the ordinary things that happen. I'm living in a grossly over-reported area. If a bomb goes off in Chicago, U.S.A., killing ten people, it will probably make news headlines in the Chicago papers and perhaps in one of the main New York papers such as the New York *Times*. And the guy sitting in England or in Moscow listening to the BBC will never hear of it. It will not make news. But if a bomb goes off in Jerusalem hitting a dog or a cat or a *sabra*, for example, it makes top news all over the world. I feel it's a gross distortion, but it's part of the facts of life.

People – all sorts, Palestinians, Israeli citizens – 'phone through all the day.

Michael Elkins is always aware that he is speaking to millions of people whenever he broadcasts.

The BBC is the only foreign news medium which is experienced every day by the many people in Israel who grew up under the Palestinian mandate and who know English. These people feel very passionately about issues, so they call me in order to get a story across. Sometimes it's used. I also receive many complaints, even from the Prime Minister's Office, as I might say sour things. As long as the complaints come in from all sides I feel alright, but every day of my life I ask myself: 'Am I being fair?'

'The children and staff are my friends'

Yvonne Mattar, 32, lives in Beit Jala near Bethlehem, where she was born. She is Headmistress of a boarding school in Beit Jala, where the children study the Jordanian curriculum.

Beit Jala is a Christian Arab town. It is thought to be the biblical Giloh, Ahithophel's home town. There are about 10,000 people living here and the town is a favourite summer resort for residents of Judea and Samaria. During the Six Day War this site provided an ideal position for the guns which shelled Jerusalem's southern suburbs.

Being a headmistress of a boarding school is a very strenuous job. My hours are very long, but, as I love my job, the time involved doesn't worry me. I don't have a husband or a family, so the children and the staff here are my friends. I get up with the children at 5.30 in the morning and then we have breakfast, followed by seven to nine periods during the day. We work and play until 8 o'clock at night. After the children go to bed, I have to prepare lessons for the next day. If I have any spare time, I might watch television or do my own studying. I like to study Arabic – my language – from the pre-Islamic period.

We teach the children Arabic (which is

The ages of the children at Yvonne's school range from four to sixteen years.

Yvonne likes to visit the port of Acre, whose history extends back thousands of years.

our language), English and Russian. The other subjects they learn are mathematics, science, history, geography, domestic science and art. This is all part of the Jordanian educational system.

There are no outdoor sports for the girls, but they do have drill.

We're an Orthodox Christian school. We pray both morning and evening, and on Sunday we go to either the Greek Church or the Russian Church.

Children start at our school at the age of four and they stay until the age of fifteen or sixteen. After that they go to high school, where they take their Jordanian matriculation. There are 158 boarders and day school students here at present. Of these, only four are boys. We're experimenting; perhaps we'll have more boys at a later stage.

I like to stay in the country for my holidays – I go to visit friends up in the north in Haifa. I love the sea and spend as much time as I can swimming in the Mediterranean. I also love to spend time in Acre, which is north of Haifa and also on the coast. Acre's history goes back to the days before the children of Israel were in Palestine. It's referred to in Egyptian records dating from about 2,000 B.C. as one of the towns that the Pharaohs conquered in their campaign against the Hittites. But archaeological discoveries point to its occupation 3,000 years before that, when primitive men using tools of stone and flint, encouraged by its fertile surroundings and natural defences, gave up a nomadic existence to make their homes here. The oldest parts of Acre are very old indeed; the newest are still raw. In many ways it's a very interesting place to visit. It's one of Israel's most colourful, if rather confusing, cities.

'The Arabs are very family-minded'

Sadia Nahhas, 25, was born in Acre and now lives with her husband and his parents in Nazareth. She works both as a pharmacist in Nazareth and as an announcer for Israeli Television in Jerusalem.

I enjoy living in Nazareth. It's beautiful, and, no matter what their religion, people can't help being aware that once Jesus was here. Not so much because of the many churches, chapels and monasteries, but because 2,000 years ago Jesus and his family really lived in Nazareth and its narrow streets. Some of those streets are not very different from the ones he wandered through as a boy.

Sadia lives with her husband's parents in a large house. The garden is full of orange trees.

Twice a week, Sadia goes to the television studios in Jerusalem to announce the news.

We live in a large Arab home with a garden full of orange and pomegranate trees. We have three bedrooms, a large living room, kitchen and a very big garden. It's normal for a working woman to help her husband pay for the upkeep of the home. The Arabs are very family-minded and since my husband is the only son in the family, he takes care both of his family and of me. I find it a bit difficult to live with them; naturally, I'd like complete privacy with my husband.

We like to invite our friends to our home – all our friends at the moment are Arabs. I love to cook, and make cakes. We love dancing of all kinds and I'm a very good belly dancer.

I studied at a university in Jerusalem. I find Jerusalem is the most beautiful city in the world. I only wish we could live there. Maybe one day we'll have children and bring them up in Jerusalem.

The city's population today is 35,000. The heart of the city is Arab-governed. Most of the citizens of Nazareth are Christian Arabs, but the Moslem minority lives among them peacefully, and the minarets of the mosques mingle with the steeples of the city's churches.

We married in a nearby village called Tarshiha, where my husband grew up. In my religion, which is Christian-Arab, it's traditional to hold parties every day of the week preceding the wedding day. The entire day of the wedding was festive, with food, drink and music until the time of the ceremony, and of course afterwards.

I work in a pharmacy every day in Afulla until one o'clock, and my television job as a news announcer is only twice a week from six o'clock until eight o'clock, when my husband drives me down to Jerusalem. I like that very much; we usually have a meal in Jerusalem or see some friends before returning home. It does make a break for us. So, it isn't difficult for me to combine both my jobs.

'Science is a major priority here'

Yehuda Lapidot is a 52-year-old professor of bio-chemistry working at the Hebrew University. He was born in Jerusalem of European parents. He has four children, one of whom is studying chemistry at the University.

I was born in Jerusalem, but my parents came from Europe. My father was from Russia and my mother from Latvia. My wife's family are sixth-generation *sabra* (Israeli).

I came back to Jerusalem from Tel Aviv before 1948 because of my activities in the Israeli underground – I was a member of the organization which fought for the liberation of Israel at the time of the British Mandate. We wanted a Jewish State, not a British Mandate here, so that Jews – mainly from Europe – could come to Israel. The British Mandate had a special law to stop immigration, the famous White Paper of 1938. So we decided to fight the British Mandate in Israel in order to establish our own State. During the war, many people were arrested and many had to move from one place to another: I had to move from Tel Aviv to Jerusalem. I stayed in Jerusalem for the War of Independence and from that time I have been a Jerusalemite.

I am a professor of bio-chemistry at the Hebrew University. I do research work

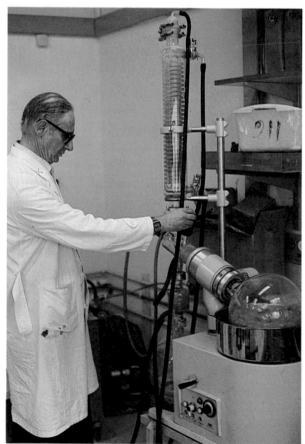

Most of Yehuda's research work is involved with the study of genetics.

48

and I teach. Most of my research is with nucleic acid, which is to do with genetics. This field is very advanced now and also very popular. I started my studies at the Hebrew University after the war of 1948. I couldn't study before then, because of the hostilities. During the war I fought against the Arabs who were then attacking Jerusalem from all sides – the Jordanian army from the east, the Egyptian army from the south and the Palestinians from all over. After the war I began regular studies, but we didn't have a university site at that time, since the Arabs had taken our university campus on Mount Scopus. So the university buildings were scattered all over the city. Much later we were able to build a new campus in Givat Ram in Jerusalem. This is where we are now.

Altogether, about 16,000 students attend the university, on several campuses. We were the first university to be established in Israel; later on in the '50s the Tel Aviv University was started; and since then others have been built round the country.

The official work hours here are 8 a.m. to 8 p.m., according to the students' lecture times. We cater for all stages of study at this university from B.Sc. to M.Sc. to Ph.D., and also post-doctorate work. But usually we encourage those who study here for Ph.D. degrees to do their post-doctorate work elsewhere. In this way they can see other laboratories and other ideas, and gain experience in other fields of work. Then, of course, they can return to our university. Those who have done their post-graduate work well return to our university and continue their work here.

In Israel, science is very highly developed when you consider the size of

Students study on the campus of the Hebrew University in front of a Henry Moore statue.

the country's population. The percentage of scientists in the population here is one of the highest in the world. There are more science students in Israel than in any country in Western Europe. We are, in fact, second only to the United States of America.

'The pages of a paper cemetery'

Benjamin Armon is a 62-year-old civil servant, Director of Commemoration and Information at Yad Vashem. His task is to keep alive the memory of those Jews who died at the hands of the Nazis in the years of the Holocaust.

I came to Israel at the age of eighteen. For the first two years I worked for Alyiah Noah, a religious movement that brought children from all over the world into Israel, or Palestine as it then was. The movement provided the children with the necessities of life and taught them how to integrate with those already living here.

Then I went to a kibbutz and was one of the founder members of Ein Hanitzviv, in the north near Bet Shean. I was there for six and a half years.

During the war I worked in the police force. Then I married and went to Jerusalem, and we started a children's home. We took in all kinds of children

This stone was erected to the memory of those one-and-a-half million Jewish children killed by the Nazis.

One of the pages of Testimony recently sent to Yad Vashem.

within the framework of Alyiah Noah. During the time I had this school I became involved with the theatre. In 1956 I was approached to help organize the annual ceremony which takes place in commemoration of the Holocaust. Once a year there's a memorial day which I organize. I knew about Yad Vashem when it was started in 1953, and became involved with its purpose. My tasks now are numerous. For example, I deal with the pages of Testimony. These are forms that are filled in by relatives or friends of those who were amongst the six million Jews who died at the hands of the Nazis in the Holocaust. As many details as possible are recorded on these pages and, in this way, the person is remembered. These pages are filed alphabetically and placed in the 'Hall of Names'. It's something like a paper cemetery: these people disappeared without trace. This is one of my most important tasks.

Young people today find it very difficult to grasp the scope of the tragedy – the annihilation of six million people and the destruction of the core of Jewish culture. Our task here at Yad Vashem is to collect information about those Jews who laid down their lives, who fought and rebelled against the Nazi enemy and his collaborators. We must perpetuate their memory and the memory of all those communities, organizations and institutions which were destroyed because they were Jewish.

One and a half million out of the six million Jews killed were children. I would like to read a poem written by a twelve-year-old girl from Nymburk called Eva Pickova. A year after she wrote this poem she was killed. It is called *Fear*.

Today the ghetto knows a different
    fear.
Close in its grip, Death wields an icy
    scythe.
An evil sickness spreads a terror in its
    wake.
The victims of its shadow weep and
    writhe.

Today a father's heartbeat tells his
    fright
And mothers bend their heads into
    their hands.
Now children choke and die with
    typhus here,
A bitter tax is taken from their bands.

My heart still beats inside my breast
While friends depart for other worlds.
Perhaps it's better – who can say? –
Than watching this, to die today?

No, no, my God, we want to live!
Not watch our numbers melt away.
We want to have a better world,
We want to work – we must not die!

51

'A school for the pioneer spirit'

Miriam Bahar is a 17-year-old member of the *Gadna*, the Israeli Youth Corps. She was born in Yok Neam, near Haifa. Her parents came from Yemen.

The *Gadna* is the Israeli Youth Corps which began its life ten years before the establishment of the State of Israel. The *Gadna* provides a national framework for teaching young people – high school students and working teenagers – the meaning of national security. It aims to give us information on security matters, to teach us good citizenship, the geogra- phy of the country, and to train us in the use and maintenance of arms for when we do our national service. We work sol- idly day and night for six days a week. It's a rough training.

Gadna *members are counted and inspected every morning in front of the Israeli flag.*

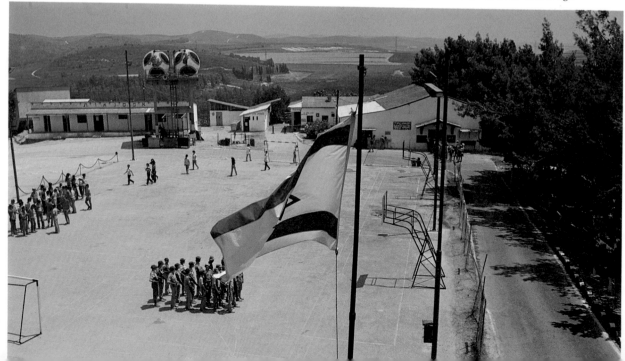

We have six bases between the mountains of Ephriam and the slopes of Carmel. Here at Jua'Ra, one of the loveliest spots in Israel, we have to get up at about 5.00 a.m. and we're then inspected and counted in front of our flag. When we've exercised for half an hour, we have to clean our rooms and be ready for breakfast at 8.00 a.m. sharp.

Usually the first activity of the day for boys and girls alike is the study of weapons – learning to use combat weapons such as the M.1 and M.16 rifles, the Kalashnikov, and the Uzzi sub-machine gun. We also have sports and self-defence lessons, with runs and hikes into the nearby countryside. We have to learn about the nature of the country, its flowers and trees.

It quite relaxing in the midst of all this to learn of our battle heritage, heroic stories that have become legends – Ben Gurion's life story, the War of Independence and so many others. Our field course studies are fun. We set up tents like scouts and learn to find our way around the area at night, using the stars as our guide.

Our morning is quite full. We break for lunch at 12.30, and then have an hour's rest before we continue our activities in the afternoon.

Then we may be taught the basics of security and guarding – how to act in emergencies in both open and closed areas, as well as standard guarding procedures such as patrols, guard duty at a gate, stopping a suspect and searching an area.

In addition to these everyday programmes, there are some three-week courses during the school summer holidays. These include navigation; *Gadna* air cadets; corporal course; dog training;

A group of Gadna *boys and girls. Dress is informal.*

and a course which teaches new immigrants our language. Apart from the bases, we have shooting clubs in various cities and sometimes we take part in competitions – even the Olympics.

We really don't have much chance to relax in the evening after a strenuous day. After dinner we have cultural activities. Then we practise night-shooting, go for night hikes, and discuss social problems.

Every high school sends its youngsters to the *Gadna*. The *Gadna* aims to prepare us to be fully-active citizens in a country burdened by unique defence problems, but working for peace and a better future. *Gadna* is not an army of youngsters: it is a school of Israel, really a school for the pioneer spirit, where volunteers can learn to serve Israel.

'We are happy and we hope for peace'

Avram Hissan, 43, was born in Bethlehem of Turkish parents. He lives above his store and factory and sells souvenirs, jewellery, olive-wood and mother-of-pearl to the many pilgrims and tourists who visit Bethlehem.

This is a magic city. It's a quiet and friendly town – not so quiet at Christmas, Easter and festivals, as thousands of pilgrims from all over the world pour into our city. Its link with the Jewish people began nearly 4,000 years ago when Jacob, passing through the town, lost his young wife Rachel in childbirth. Bethlehem today has a population of 32,000 – mainly Christian Arabs with professions. Many of them are goldsmiths, skilled in carving. Every visitor is attracted to the Church of the Nativity, traditionally the birthplace of Jesus, where Mary gave birth and laid the child in the manger because there was no room for him in the inn. The Church of the Nativity is one of the holiest shrines in Christendom.

For many generations now we've sold articles carved in olive wood and also goods made of mother-of-pearl. They are the most sought-after goods in Bethlehem, extremely popular with the tourists. The olive-wood industry is famous here. We have our own factory beneath

A craftsman works with olive wood in Avram Hissan's factory.

our store where we make all kinds of figures and nativity sets. The majority of the olive-wood goods sold in the store are made on the premises.

We call olive wood the holy wood. We carve very large pieces too – large 'manger sets' are bought and taken all over the world, especially at Christmas time.

Thank God, without religion we cannot live. I pray in St. Mary's Church in Bethlehem. Our services are held in the Aramaic language in our churches all over the world. This was the language of the Lord Our Saviour, and of our Prophets, Abraham, Isaac and Jacob.

I work in the store every day from 8 o'clock until 7 or 8 o'clock in the evening. On Sundays I go to church in the morning and then go into work. I like to take holidays, but only a day at a time. I usually go with my brother George. I like to go in and around Bethlehem, sometimes to King Solomon's Pools. This is one of our main beauty spots; it's fertile and the pool is spring-fed by the Tahunat wadi. It was erected some 500 years ago, and is now ringed by a well-grown pine forest. These great open reservoirs form a green and beautiful park. an ideal picnic spot.

I also like to go to Jericho and to the Dead Sea where the climate is much warmer and dryer than here. I'm very much a family man and I enjoy staying at home in the evenings with my family; so many friends come in to visit us and, of course, business people, mainly from the United States.

Christians and Moslems live together in Bethlehem. We have very good relations with the Jews; we have lived together now for fourteen years. We are happy and we hope for peace in the future.

'Bringing back animals from biblical times'

Avraham Yoffee is a 67-year-old nature preservationist. His aim is to restock Israel with some of the animals mentioned in the Bible. He lives in Ramat HaSharon with his wife and three children.

I'm based in an office in Tel Aviv but I spend very little time there. I was born and raised on a farm, and at the age of fourteen attended an agricultural school, so I was used to being out on the land. That has never changed. In those days, my natural-history teacher made a great impression on me. His influence has stayed with me and I'm sure he would be pleased to know what I am doing today. In 1964, just out of the army, I looked around for a civilian job and was asked to set up a nature reserve and national park authority.

I wanted time to save, conserve and protect whatever remained of nature's history of flora and fauna in our country. My main job is to protect not only flowers, trees, animals and birds in the

A group of White Oryx at rest on the Yotvata Nature Reserve.

reserve, but also those outside the reserve. At the beginning I had only two men to help me; now we have about 250, rangers and scientists. We have a network of men all over the country who are enforcing the law, preventing people from uprooting flowers, cutting down trees, and shooting animals, birds and so on.

We find a large tract of land – 500, 10,000 or even 25,000 acres (200, 4,000 or 10,000 ha) – and ask the government if we can use it for a national park. If they agree, they pass a law to prohibit any commercial development on that land. If anyone abuses this law, he is either arrested or fined very heavily. We ourselves act as officers of the law and have the authority to stop people breaking this law.

This is an independent project under the umbrella of the nature reserve. It's not government-sponsored. We call it the *Hibar*. Down south, in the Arava depression, animals still roam wild as they did in biblical times. The Yotvata Nature Reserve, as it is called, is a wildlife game park of 8,500 acres (3,500 ha). We developed it in a setting of natural beauty for animals like the oryx, the gazelle and the ibex. The oryx is the animal which started the legend of the unicorn. The Arabian oryx had two horns, but looked at from the side view, it seemed only to have one horn. Hence the legend of the unicorn.

Then there is the wild ass which was mentioned in the Bible, but has since become extinct. This country is a land-bridge between three continents, Africa in the south, Europe in the north and Asia in the east. Every power that wanted to control part of this country had to cross Israel. This played havoc

An ibex stands elegant amidst the rugged beauty of the wild-life game park.

with chances of survival of the animals, mainly the large ones. At the present time we don't have many of the animals mentioned in the Bible, so I aim to bring some of them back to Israel. At first I'll put them in enclosures, where they will be able to reproduce in a protected environment. Then I'll set some free in the desert.

I travel all over the world, collecting animals wherever I can. It's a long, hard job. My wardens are trying, by controlled breeding, to revive species which were once a common sight here, as many of the Bible's most poetic passages testify. Throughout Israel, there are some 120 areas which have been set aside as nature reserves in which landscape, flora and fauna are protected.

'The average Israeli can't afford a taxi'

Eli Shalgi is a 34-year-old taxi driver. He lives in Gilo on the outskirts of Jerusalem. He is fifth-generation Israeli of Greek descent. Like most taxi drivers in Israel, he is finding that inflation is reducing his earnings drastically.

I've been a taxi driver for just over eight years now. I began after the Yom Kippur War in 1973. I work a very long day, anything from twelve to eighteen hours. I like to go home in the middle of the day for two hours so that I can see my children. When I get home late at night they're already asleep. Here in Israel most people take time off at midday because of the climate – it's very hot, especially in the summer months.

My only day of relaxation is Saturday, which is our Sabbath. Here in Israel we don't have a 'week-end'; we all work a six-day week. If I can, I love to go to a football match on my day off. Sometimes on a Saturday, we go down to the Dead

Eli's next passenger is unlikely to be an Israeli: the average Israeli cannot afford the high fares.

Sea and picnic amongst the papyrus grasses and the springs. The Dead Sea is well-known to visitors: its hot springs and the minerals in its water cure many ailments.

I have to speak several languages – Ivrit (Israeli), English, a little French, German and Arabic – most important since a third of the population are Arabs.

I'm only allowed to carry four passengers in my car. Most of my passengers are tourists, from all over the world, and a few are Israelis. I say a few because charges are so high that the average Israeli can't afford a taxi; they might use a bus or *sharoot* instead. A *sharoot* is a large limousine that takes seven people. There are special stations where you can pick one up to travel from station A to station B. Sometimes you can be dropped off *en route*. You have to buy a ticket, just as you would buy a train ticket. They run every half hour throughout the day until midnight. I would charge 900 shekels in comparison with seventy shekels for the same journey in a *sharoot*.

Taxi drivers here are finding that their earnings are decreasing rapidly. Inflation is a big problem, particularly in winter months when there are no tourists around, or very few. Now it's even too expensive for the average person to take a taxi for a short journey. And we are taxed very highly.

It was very easy to become a taxi driver fifteen years ago. Consequently we now have many taxi drivers who are old. This is bad both for the tourists and for us. The law shouldn't allow these old people to hold licences now. Perhaps licences should only be valid for a certain length of time.

A few years ago a terrorist attacked a

The papyrus grasses which grow in Ein Feshha, by the Dead Sea.

taxi driver, killed him and left him in the boot of his car. This was the first of several incidents, so now ninety-five per cent of taxi drivers carry a gun if they're driving in the area of the West Bank or in Arab areas.

I really love driving out into the country. Our country is so small. Since the Six Day War of 1967, the total area under Israeli administration, including Israel itself, has extended from the Golan Heights in the north, to Sharm el Sheikh in the south. We are bounded in the north by Lebanon and Syria; in the east by the Jordan River; and in the south-west by the Gulf of Suez and the Suez Canal. All-told, the land area of Israel is 89,359 square kilometres (34,502 square miles), of which only 20,700 square kilometres (7,992 square miles) made up Israel as it was before June 1967. You see, it really is a very small country, and to show people our countryside – the Galilee and Golan, and then the complete contrast of the Negev and Sinai, the desert areas – is the most exciting way to spend my days.

'Excavating the landmarks of tomorrow'

Meir Ben-Dor was born 45 years ago in Metulla, in the north of Israel. His family came from Russia. Educated in Jerusalem as an archaeologist, his ambition is to create an archaeological park in Jerusalem.

I took part in excavations as a student – later I directed the excavations at Belvoir, which is a crusader castle near Bet Shean. I came here to Jerusalem in 1968 and worked around the Temple Mount, at the beginning as an assistant and for the last three years directing the dig.

We're now on the highest side of the city where most of the Judean Palaces used to be. We're looking for the remains of those palaces. Last year we discovered

Remains of the water system of buildings of the Second Temple period.

some remains of walls and this summer we're going to enlarge the area of our search and hope to find more from that period.

I've been working here exactly thirteen years. My day starts at 7.00 a.m. I give the workers their instructions and guide them through their day and we finish around 3.00 p.m. – some of the workers finish much later, at 5.00 p.m. This is the usual pattern of my day, with the exception of Saturdays and Mondays.

For some of my holidays I go abroad to Europe – Italy, Spain or Greece, where I visit archaeological sites. I have learnt so much on my travels. It is particularly interesting to see archaeological reconstructions and sites which have been preserved: all this is important for my work here. When I'm in Israel I don't take holidays. I have to do my reserve army service, *Millouin* as we call it.

At my age, a man has to give forty-five days a year to *Millouin*. This is spread over the year. I work in the educational side of the army, giving lectures to soldiers on the historical background of the country. So I have to travel all over Israel.

Digging is the past. For the future, we want to open this site as an archaeological park. It will be most unusual, because the history of Jerusalem is unusual. We have here a story of twenty-five different periods, and we're arranging the park so that people will have a feeling of those twenty-five different periods. People walk along the city wall; they visit a crusader tower; they go to an Aslamic Palace or a Byzantine Villa. So they will come to visit the remains of the Judean Palaces. The sites we are excavating today will be the landmarks of tomorrow.

Workers digging at the Dung Gate of Jerusalem's Old City Wall.

Facts

Capital city: Jerusalem.

Principal language: Hebrew. Arabic is spoken by the ½ million Arab minority as well as by the population of the 'occupied areas'. Many European languages are also spoken.

Currency: The shekel was introduced in 1980. It equals 10 Israeli pounds and is worth about 4.8p or 10 U.S. cents.

Religions: Judaism; there are two main Jewish communities – *Ashkenazim* and *Sephardim*. Also Moslems, Christians, and Druzes.

Population: 3,799,900 (1979). In 1969 the Jewish population in Israel constituted about 18 per cent of the estimated total Jewish population of the world. Over 80 per cent of the population live in urban areas. Over one-third live within a 25-mile (40-km) radius of Tel Aviv. The population is growing rapidly because of immigration. 4 per cent live in *moshavim* (co-operative small-holders' villages); 3 per cent live in *kibbutzim*; 2 per cent are transient – isolated or nomadic bedouin.

Climate: Climatic conditions vary between regions. Mainly Mediterranean climate – hot, dry summers; mild, rainy winters.

Government: Israel is an independent sovereign republic with a one-chamber parliament, the Knesset. The Knesset consists of 120 members elected for 4 years by secret ballot and universal adult suffrage. The President is constitutional head of state, elected by the Knesset for 5 years. The Cabinet has executive powers and is led by a Prime Minister. Israel is divided into 6 administrative districts. Local Authorities are elected every 4 years. There are 31 municipal corporations, 115 local councils and 49 regional councils (in agricultural areas).

Housing: Housing has been a major call on investment resources. In 1976 an estimated 28,500 families lived in sub-standard housing. Between 1960 and 1967 642,420 new housing units were built, allocated mainly to new immigrants. Prefabrication and other labour-saving methods of construction are common.

Education: 1 in every 3 Israelis is a student. Free, compulsory education for children aged 5–16 years. Free education until age of 18 years. Unified state-controlled elementary school system. There are private schools, schools maintained by municipalities, and schools administered by teachers' co-operatives or trustees. Parents may choose between state lay or state religious education. There is secondary vocational, technical, agricultural and maritime training. Israel has 40 teacher training colleges; 6 universities; 1 institute of technology; and 1 graduate school of science. Satellite colleges have been established to make higher education more accessible in outlying areas.

Military service: Compulsory for all men between the ages of 18 and 29 for 36 months; for some unmarried women between 18 and 26 for 24 months. After their term of military service, men and childless women are on reserve until the ages of 55 and 34 respectively.

Agriculture: Valley of Jezreel is the main agricultural centre. Particular features of Israeli agriculture include: kibbutzim – collective settlements where all profits and earnings are collectively owned and work is collectively organized; irrigation schemes – skilful use made of scarce water resources; reclamation of the Negev desert. Main produce: olives, tobacco, citrus fruits, grapes. Also fish breeding and poultry raising. Except for cereals, beef, sugar and some animal foods, Israel grows most of its food requirements.

Industry: Manufactured, processed and finished products include: chemicals, metal products, textiles, tyres, paper, plastics, leather goods, glass, ceramics, construction materials, precision instruments and electric goods. Israel is second only to Belgium in the processing of diamonds for the world market.

The Media: Israel has 27 daily newspapers (including 13 Hebrew and 4 Arabic). There is no local press. Few dailies are economically self-supporting: most depend on subsidies. The Israeli television service is broadcast from Jerusalem and is controlled by the Israel Broadcasting Authority. Programmes are in Hebrew and Arabic. Half the schedules are reserved for educational programmes. Radio broadcasts are also controlled by the Israel Broadcasting Authority. There are 5 programmes for local and overseas listeners in 13 languages.

Index

Abraham 11, 15, 28, 55
absorption centre 36
Abuiack tribe 14
Acre 45
Affula 47
AGREXO 25
Allenby Bridge 30
Alyiah Noah 50
Aramaic language 55
Arava depression 57
archaeology 45, 60–61

BBC 42
bedouins 14–15, 27; tent 14
Beersheba 8
Beit Jala 44
Beit Shearim 60
Belvoir 60
Ben Gurion 9, 53;
    University 8–9
Bethlehem 54
Bet Shean 50

camels 15; clinic for 41
Carmel 52
Church of the Nativity 54
climate 27, 29
community service 7
copper mines 28

Damascus 27
David, King of Israel 29
Dead Sea 11, 23, 55, 58
Diaspora Yeshiva 34
drip irrigation 7

ebony 27
Edom 23
Egypt 39
Eichman, Adolf 38
Ein Hanitzviv 50
Ein Karem 11, 33
El Al Israeli Airlines 22–3

El-Aqsa Mosque 27
epidemiology 40
Eshkol, Levi 38
excavations, archaeological 60

flora and fauna 56

Gadna, the 20–21, 52–3
Galilee 59; Sea of 23
Gate of Mercy 35
Gaza 21
genetics 49
Gethsemane, Garden of 11
Giloh 44
Gimorah 35
Givat Ram 49
Golan Heights 59
Golden Gate 35
Golgotha 11
'green revolution', the 7

Haifa 23, 39, 45
Hall of Names 51
Hebrew University 49
Hebron 11, 27
Herod 19
Hibar, the 57
Holocaust, the 7, 51
'Holy Fire', day of the 16
Holy Sepulchre 11, 17

immigrants 9, 12–13, 22–3, 42,
    53
inflation 59
Isaac 28, 55
Israel Museum 29

Jacob 28, 54, 55
Jaffa 11, 39
Jericho 11, 18, 19, 23, 27, 55
Jerusalem 11, 21, 23, 26, 32,
    34, 36, 39, 43, 44, 47, 48, 49,
    50, 60

Jesus Christ 11, 16, 46, 54, 55
Jewish Agency, the 36, 37
Jezreel Valley 24, 28
Jonathan 29
Jordan 18, 30; educational
    system of 45; River 28, 30,
    59
Jua'Ra 52
Judgement Gate 11

kibbutzim 6–7, 23, 28, 50
King Solomon's Pools 55

'Margic Carpet', operation 22,
    42
Mandate, British 39, 43, 48
markets 27
Mary, Virgin 54
Mediterranean Sea 23, 45
Meir, Golda 38
Messiah, the 35
military service 39
Millouin 61
Mohammed 27
Monastery of St. George 19
Mosad, the 38
moshavim 23
Moslems 15, 47, 55
mother-of-pearl 27, 55
Mount Carmel 28
Mount Gilboa 28
Mount of Olives 11, 35
Mount Scopus 49

national park 57; authority 56
national service 39, 52
Nazareth 46
Nazis 38, 51
Negev desert 20, 28, 59
nomads 14–15

olive wood 55
'open apartments' 9

63

Index – cont.

palaces, Judean 60
Palestine 11, 38, 45
Parliament (Knesset) 38
Pharaohs, the 45
pine forests 25
police 50
Prophets, the 17, 23, 55

Rachel 54

Samaria 44
schools 10, 44–5
scout movement 6, 21
sculpture 28
Sharm el Sheikh 59
Sinai desert 13, 59
Six Day War, the 32, 44, 59
social work 13, 37
sport 45, 52
Suez Canal 59
Suez, Gulf of 59

Talmud the 35
Tarshiha 47
Tel Aviv 20, 23, 39, 48, 56
television 13
Temple, the 35
Temple Mount 60
Testimony 51
'Tomb of the Lord', the 17
Torah 35
tourists 27, 31, 55, 58

Ulpan 37
underground, Israeli 48
United Nations 17

veterinary medicine 40
violence 43

Wadi Faran 11
Wadi Kelt 18
War of Independence 38, 42,
   48, 53
West Bank, the 21, 30, 39, 59
wildlife 41

Yad Vashem 51
Yom Kippur War 58
Yotvasha Nature Reserve 57

Zionist 43

Glossary

absorption centre A settlement where new immigrants are taught about the culture and geography of Israel.

bedouin A member of a nomadic tribe.

cross-breeding Breeding plants using parents of different varieties.

British Mandate The responsibility conferred on Britain by the League of Nations to control and administer Palestine. This came to an end with Israel's independence in 1948.

ecological system The harmony between living things and their environment.

epidemiology The branch of medical science concerned with widespread diseases.

genetics The study of heredity and variation in living things.

Gemara Part of the *Talmud* (see below).

Holocaust The mass murder by the Nazis in the Second World War of the Jews and other 'unwanted' populations at extermination centres.

kibbutz **(pl. -im)** A collective agricultural settlement owned and administered by its members.

moshav **(pl. -im)** A co-operative settlement consisting of a number of small farms.

nomad A member of a people or tribe which moves from place to place in search of food or pasture.

Ramadan The thirty days in which Moslems fast from sunrise to sunset.

sabra A Jew born in Israel.

Six Day War The war in which Israel defeated Egypt, Jordan and Syria during June 1967.

Talmud The book of Jewish law and tradition.

Torah The body of the Jewish sacred writings and traditions.

Zionist A supporter of the development of Israel as a national homeland for Jews.